ON THE CONTRARY

Oscar Wilde & Friedrich Nietzsche

Yahia Lababidi

Fomite
Burlington, VT

ISBN: 978-1-967022-14-4

Fomite
58 Peru Street
Burlington, VT 05401
www.fomitepress.com

10-11-2025

Contents

The Great Contrarians

The externals of their lives could not have been more different. One was a celebrated wit and dramatist, the other a reclusive philosopher who, throughout his conscious life, lived and wrote in relative obscurity. Yet to varying extents, and with varying results, both thought of themselves as poets. Both, also in their way, concerned themselves with founding a philosophy grounded in the art of living, turning to antiquity (Ancient Greece) for their ideal, and considering contemporary France the accepted heir to their sensual sophistication. Natural provocateurs, they were incorrigible cultural agitators, and reserved some of their most withering criticism for their 'so-called countrymen'. Ultimately, both were regarded as the premier stylists of their time (late 1800s) and said as much. Although contemporaries, they were probably unaware of each other, yet came to embody in their flamboyant personae and utterances the tensions and antagonisms of *fin de siècle* Europe.

"The two great turning points in my life," Oscar Wilde wrote in *De Profundis*, "were when my father sent me to Oxford, and when society sent me to prison." In between those two great turning points, Wilde's career was a series of smaller ones. As a brilliant classicist, he graduated with First Class Honors, having won the prestigious Newdigate Prize for Poetry; previous winners included luminaries such as John Ruskin and Matthew Arnold. He later came to be more closely associated with the Aesthetic Movement, whose doctrine 'Art for Art's sake' was espoused by his Oxford professor and art critic, Walter

Pater. Wilde then went about making a name for himself through extravagant dress and conversation before he had written a book, fulfilling a prophesy he'd made to one of his Oxford friends: "Somehow or other I'll be famous and if not famous, I'll be notorious."

Years later, Wilde addressed a question that plagued him early on—'But what has Mr. Oscar Wilde *done?*'—in his only novel, *The Picture of Dorian Gray*, "The mere fact of having published a book of second-rate sonnets makes a man quite irresistible. He lives the poetry that he cannot write." By then, Wilde had already published his book of second-rate verse. But this controversial novel was preceded by a reputation-establishing lecture tour of North America and followed by a collection of arresting essays, as well as a string of successful plays that best showcased his peculiar comedic genius. By the time of his arrest for homosexual "sodomy", Wilde was at the peak of his powers, having conquered literary London one dinner table at a time, personifying a witty and amoral philosophy that was, in the astute observation of contemporary Irish playwright Bernard Shaw, 'Nietzschean…Beyond Good and Evil.'

The son of a Lutheran minister, Friedrich Nietzsche was a precocious child, nicknamed the "little pastor" for his demeanor and discipline. Yet, by the time he was accepted to a Chair of Philology at the unusual age of 24, and exceptionally awarded a doctorate degree without examination, the brilliant young linguist was already protesting the existence of a Christian God, and would continue protesting for the remainder of his adult life. Moreover, the artist in him was too pronounced to sit well with the academic community. Instead, Nietzsche, a minor composer, came to regard Wagner as his model; and was drawn into intimate contact with the master who, like him, was devoted to the pessimist philosopher Schopenhauer, and a fellow Romantic. Alas, this was not to last. In a life marked by overcoming, Wagner and Schopenhauer were soon overthrown.

Mounting disenchantment with academia and deteriorating health (persistent migraines and nausea) compelled Nietzsche to resign his professorship. "How useless and arbitrary my whole existence as a philologist appeared in relation to my task. I felt ashamed of this *false* modesty … crawling scrupulously with bad eyes through ancient metrists," he says to himself in his astonishing autobiography, *Ecce Homo* ("Behold the Man"). For the next decade he proceeded to 'recall and reflect' on himself, leading a life of solitary wandering, and produced a striking collection of intellectually provocative and stylistically remarkable books that served to establish him as one of the most influential philosophers of the nineteenth century.

Even though hardly read, Nietzsche seems to have been thoroughly assured of his merits, prophesying that someday professorships would be dedicated exclusively to his philosophy, which would in turn alter the fate of Europe. Referring to himself as a Destiny, he reconciled himself to his lack of renown with his formula, "some are born posthumously." However, when the universal fame he so craved came, he was cruelly excluded from it, mentally insane for the last decade of his life. The man presented to the world in his works, while certainly less willfully superficial than Wilde, was nevertheless just as rich in masks and contradictions.

"Questions are never indiscreet," quipped Wilde in *An Ideal Husband*, "answers sometimes are." In such matters, a small curiosity is petty, while a great curiosity is philosophic. Both Wilde and Nietzsche were profoundly inquisitive spirits, intrepid seekers, asking deep and difficult questions of their time and culture. Nietzsche termed this: *Revaluation of all Values*, a concept and practice Wilde was not at all unfamiliar with, one that entailed a relentless interrogation of moral prejudices, revealing weaknesses where others alleged strength, with vice posing as virtue. Again, Nietzsche in *The Antichrist*, may as well be speaking for Wilde when he says: "We free spirits are already a revaluation of values, an incarnate declaration of war against the old concepts of 'true' and 'untrue'. This declaration of war, 'without powder and smoke…without pathos and strained limbs', as Nietzsche wrote in his autobiography, was waged on two millennia of humanity, or Western Civilization, no less.

As artist-thinkers they were revolutionary and subversive in their distrust of prejudices, smashing idols and tablets of unexamined convictions, in the belief that creators of new values must also be destroyers of old ones.

In the *The Case of Wagner*, Nietzsche defines the philosopher as "the evil consciousness of his age". Both he and Wilde made it their self-appointed task to disclose to their own age its hypocrisies. In his essay "The Soul of Man under Socialism", Wilde had written: "As one reads history…one is absolutely sickened, not by the crimes that the wicked have committed, but by the punishments that the good have inflicted." And, in the preface of *Dorian Gray*, Wilde drives the point home: "The nineteenth century dislike of realism is the rage of Caliban [Shakespeare's bestial man in *The Tempest*] seeing his own face in a glass." In doing so, throughout their different careers, both thinkers launched scathing attacks on their respective homelands, Germany and England, employing comedy and contempt for their weapons and armor.

Considering himself "condemned to Germans" Nietzsche coined the term "cultural philistines" to describe the Fatherland that he felt contaminated every culture it touched, and had on its conscience every crime against culture committed in the last four centuries. Increasingly, in his mouth, the word "German" became a term of abuse. And, in the final equation, there was simply 'too much beer in the German intellect'. Wilde used a similar put-down with regard toEngland. In *Dorian Gray* (termed "the first French novel to be written in the English language") Lord Henry posing as Oscar Wilde, wickedly remarks: "Beer, the Bible, and the seven deadly virtues have made our England what she is." "Beer" is shorthand for what is crude and unrefined. The antidote to mediocrity or vulgarity lay in France. For Nietzsche, whose conceit was that he was a 'good European' and that he *conceived* his work in French, Germans were 'clumsy and rectangular' versus Parisian 'nuance and mosaic'. Wilde, who railed against the morally stifling atmosphere

9

of Victorian England, threatened to renounce
his British nationality in favor of becoming a
naturalized French citizen when his attempt
to stage in London his Symbolist play *Salome*
(translated from the French) was thwarted
by censorship.

In literature, content dictates form, and it
is not without significance that Wilde and
Nietzsche both expressed themselves in
similar forms—aphorisms, epigrams and
maxims. These were forms practically invented
by the Greek pre-Socratic philosophers, and
mastered by the French moralists. Vast
thoughts condensed could be transmitted
through these deceptively slight vessels which
relied on the culture of the reader to release
them. Moreover, their pithy phrasing ensured
they were memorable. Nietzsche writes in
Thus Spoke Zarathustra: "Whoever writes
in blood and aphorisms does not want to
be read but to be learned by heart. In the
mountains the shortest way is from peak to

peak: but for that one must have long legs. Aphorisms should be peaks—and those who are addressed, tall and lofty." Whoever writes in aphorisms, then, must be possessed of great ambition and economy of style. Elsewhere, in *Twilight of the Idols*, Nietzsche puts it this way: "Aphorisms in which I am the first master among Germans, are the forms of "eternity"; my ambition is to say in ten sentences what everyone else says in a book—what everyone else does not say in a book." As a stylist, Nietzsche felt he was so good he spoiled the tastes of his readers, since they could enjoy no one after him, and that along with the poet Heine, he would be regarded as the greatest stylist in the German language; he later added Goethe to this exclusive list.

Wilde shared this incredibly high estimate of himself and ambition, declaring his genius to all who would listen (once famously to a US customs official in answer to the standard question: 'do you have anything to declare') "I have nothing to declare but my genius". "Our proverbs want rewriting," he had written in *Dorian Gray*, and he set about doing so over the span of his career in oft-repeated epigrams and maxims (with titles like: "*A Few Maxims for the Instruction of the Overeducated, or Phrases and Philosophies for the Use of the Young*"). In his long prison letter, *De Profundis*, he surveyed his lifework, approvingly: "I had summed up all systems in a sentence and existence in an epigram." But, braggadocio aside, it is astounding how nearly indistinguishable some of their aphorisms are, almost interchangeable in form and substance. For example:

What fire does not destroy, it hardens.
— Wilde

What does not kill me makes me stronger.
— Nietzsche

The simple truth, is that not a double lie?
— Nietzsche

The truth is rarely pure and never simple.
— Wilde

Public opinion exists only where there are no ideas.
— Wilde

To say it again, Public opinions, private laziness.
— Nietzsche

We possess art lest we perish of the truth.
— Nietzsche

The telling of beautiful untrue things is the proper aim of art.
— Wilde

Conscience and cowardice are really the same thing.
— Wilde

Not to perpetrate cowardice against one's own acts! ... The bite of conscience is indecent.
— Nietzsche

Discontent is the first step in the progress of a man or nation.
— Wilde

Every great progress must be preceded by a partial weakening.
— Nietzsche

These are heavy words lightly thrown, intended not so much to reveal the writer/speaker, as to establish a persona. Interestingly, the etymology of persona—*per* meaning through and *sona* meaning sound—literally means to *sound through*, because Greek actors sounded through *"a mask"* (which is what a persona is). 'Give a man a mask and he shall tell you the truth,' agrees Oscar Wilde in his Platonic dialogue: *The Critic as Artist*. Nietzsche, too, admits: "Every profound spirit needs a mask" and "talking much about oneself can also be a means to conceal oneself."

One would think it near impossible to navigate such a moral universe that is without constants or compass, yet this is not so. Surprising but inevitably, the seemingly disparate personas Wilde and Nietzsche created and sent out into the world, came to spell out a coherent (albeit fluid) philosophy. What's more, these crowded personas shared many key features.

Matters of Style

One of the central tenets that both Nietzsche and Wilde's philosophies pivoted upon was the importance of style. In an aphorism titled, *One Thing Is Needful*, Nietzsche states his strategy. "To give style" to one's character—a great and rare art! He exercises it who surveys all that his nature presents in strength and weakness and then molds it to an artistic plan until everything appears as art and reason, and even the weaknesses delight the eye. Elsewhere, Nietzsche writes: "improving our style means improving our ideas, and nothing else."

For Wilde, too, style and substance were inseparable, and in matters of great or slight importance, style was paramount. Moreover, Wilde innately understood this art of being and becoming;'giving style to one's character' or self-fashioning was for him second nature. In "Phrases and Philosophies for the Use of the Young", Wilde writes: "One should either be a work of art, or wear a work of art." Whichever the case proved to be, he and Nietzsche presented themselves with great flair and wore their learning lightly; their deep erudition and delineation of perceptions seamlessly transformed into something quite poetic.

To accommodate their multidimensional personalities, both employed a multidimensional style, prompting their detractors to refer to them as the most 'uneven of great writers'. As antinomians, opposed to the obligatoriness of the moral law, it was thus for "stylistic" reasons that both borrowed Biblical thunder and cadences—Nietzsche for his *Zarathustra*, Wilde in *Salome*—adapting scriptural phraseology to suit their peculiar temperaments. It is worthwhile to note that they both held inordinately high views of both these works. Wilde was more proud of *Salome* ('this scarlet piece which I in some strange mood wrote') than any of his other plays, and Nietzsche unequivocally declared *Zarathustra* the 'greatest gift to mankind.'

Philosophically, Nietzsche christened his approach, *The Gay Science*, also translated as *Joyful Wisdom*. Essentially, it is a worldview in praise of lightheartedness or *esprit* (witty intelligence) with 'light feet' and 'wit' for leitmotifs. Wilde shared in this playful philosophy which advocated exuberance, buoyancy and a sustaining sunny humor (though both were not averse to a little playful malice, as well). In the famous catchphrase of another heavyweight with great style, boxing champion Muhammed Ali, they could "float like a butterfly, sting like a bee." Coincidentally, Wilde's *Importance of Being Earnest*, a play bristling with stinging wit, was written as the author told a friend, "by a butterfly for butterflies." The biting light touch was a specialty of theirs, and a style which they utilized to great effect.

Despite occasional cynicism, their greatest art of living was their impulse to be joyful. Together with this, they both retained to a high degree the childlike faculties of wonder, joy, and belief in the impossible. This is evidenced in any of Wilde's many improbable utterances (or his delightful

persona with its boyish immaturity) as much
as in his enchanting short stories for children.
Argentine poet and author, Jorge Luis Borges,
who generally admired Wilde's work, also
spoke of his 'invulnerable innocence'. In
Nietzsche, we see it in the central role he
assigned to the child in *Zarathustra*; after
becoming first a camel (beast of burden),
and then a preying lion, the birth of the
child is the final metamorphosis of the spirit.
"Innocence is the child, and forgetfulness,
a new beginning, a game, a self-propelling
wheel," he says in *Zarathustra*. Elsewhere,
in *Beyond Good and Evil*, Nietzsche defines
mature manhood as: "that means to have
rediscovered the seriousness one had as
a child at play." Along with innocence,
Nietzsche and Wilde's child also represented
irreverence, a sense of fun, and the license
also to poke fun. "Not by wrath, but by
laughter do we slay. Come, let us slay the
spirit of gravity." Thus spake Nietzsche's

Zarathustra. In a letter, Nietzsche puts it still more mischievously 'I hang a little farcical tail on to the most serious things.' This is a sensibility that is amply echoed in Wilde: 'Life is too important to be taken seriously' (*Lady Windermere's Fan*) or the countless instances of trivializing seriousness that litter his work. Priding himself on his ability to stroke prickly subjects, Nietzsche suggests in the *The Gay Science* "It is best to do with profound problems as with a cold bath quickly in, quickly out." To extend the simile, this is the attitude of the dolphin that plummets to the depths, then breaks the surface with an acrobatic display. Nietzsche summarizes this tendency in an epitaph to one of his latest books, *The Case of Wagner* (1888): "Through what is laughable say what is somber." In the final equation, their answer to 'profound problems' was a stylistic one (aesthetics over ethics) and to achieve this, they often found it necessary to return to the surface of things.

World of Appearances

Above all, Nietzsche and Wilde were great lovers of life, anachronistic Greeks in their adoration of the sun (as life-force) and their heady vitalist philosophies, sensually imbued with this-world spirituality, with Beauty for its (visible) Ideal. Likewise, in their deep belief in the wisdom of the body, they echoed the Greek Ideal of the dependence of a healthy mind on a healthy body.

Oh, those Greeks! They knew how to live. What is required for that is to stop courageously at the surface, the fold, the skin, to adore appearances, to believe in forms, tones, words, in the whole Olympus of appearance. Those Greeks were superficial— out of profundity.

This is not Wilde waxing poetic, but Nietzsche philosophic. Of course, this is also the very same Aesthetic philosophy Wilde championed: "It is only shallow people who do not judge by appearances" (*Picture of Dorian Gray*). Moreover, refinement and taste were aesthetic virtues both prized. "All of life is a dispute over taste and tasting," Nietzsche has Zarathustra say. Such an aesthetic philosophy was not only an interpretation of life, but a guide or philosophy for life. This is why they turned to those Greeks, for "they knew how to live." Nietzsche and Wilde may have also been 'superficial out of profundity' in yet another way, if we allow that their preference for appearances may have been informed by Kantian skepticism, as propounded in his *Critique of Pure Reason* (1781). According to this doctrine, we never know things as they are, but only as they *appear* to be, hence their resolve to 'stop courageously at the surface', in this context, might not seem unwise.

On another level, "aestheticism" according

to Alexander Nehamas' study of Nietzsche: *Life as Literature*, entailed a tendency to view the world in general as a work of art, or as a literary text in particular, with people, including himself, as literary characters populating it; or an essential reliance on an artistic model for understanding and evaluating the world and people. This is to say, reading and writing were Nietzsche's models for living and loving, and that he lived for and through the written word, as well as learned from and argued with books. As Nehamas writes of Nietzsche's aestheticism, "therefore, his use of and emphasis on style, is itself part of his effort to undermine the distinction between form and content in life as well as writing."

Merging life with literature was second nature to Wilde, who openly admitted to performing his life. Complimenting an actor who played the lead in a comedy of his, Wilde quipped: "...everyday [he] becomes *de plus en plus Oscarisé.*" Or to Andre Gide, "My life is like a work of art; an artist never starts the same thing twice." What's more, he felt Life imitated Art far more than vice versa. And although as a wit about town, he certainly got out more than the reclusive Nietzsche, he confessed in *De Profundis*: "I treated art as the supreme reality and life as a mere mode of fiction." Or, as he has Gilbert argue in *The Critic as Artist*: "When a man acts he is a puppet, when he describes he is a poet." Within this verbal universe, denying free will and affirming the supremacy of language, there is much of Nietzsche, reclaiming power from a mute fate only through eloquent and articulate expression.

In Nietzsche, we have the philosopher as performance artist, communicating in jokes, riddles, parables, poems, songs, or aphorisms. In *Ecce Homo*, he suggests this himself: "I desire no 'believers,' I think I am too malicious even to believe in myself…I

have no wish to be a saint, I would rather
be a buffoon…Perhaps I am a buffoon."
In Wilde, it is the artist as performing
philosopher, having made as he wrote in his
famous letter from prison, *De Profundis*, "art
a philosophy and philosophy an art." Or, in
the uncharacteristically lavish praise of the
cantankerous Shaw: "In a certain sense Mr.
Wilde is to me our only thorough playwright.
He plays with everything: with wit, with
philosophy, with drama, with actors and
audience, with the whole theatre." Following
his friend's death, Max Beerbohm—critic
and caricaturist—estimates Wilde's legacy
such: "He came as a thinker, a weaver of
ideas…Theatrical construction, sense of
theatrical effects, were his by instinct."

Nietzsche and Wilde could have said,
with Blake, "I must create a system or
be enslaved by another man's." Stainless
individualists and sublime egoists, the two of
them preached a hedonistic individualism,

prescribing self-love, and selfish virtues in the interest of self-realization, which they felt was the aim of life. Towards this aim, both wrote in praise of idleness, or the hard work of doing nothing, save musing. In the *Critic as Artist*, Wilde found people 'overworked and undereducated'. In *Phrases and Philosophies for the Use of the Young*, he extolled the virtue of idleness as a "condition of perfection" and preached idleness as an 'exquisite art'. Being idle is very hard work, he lamented, because everyone is against you. Meanwhile, Nietzsche describes his *Twilight of the Idols*, as "an escapade into the idle hours of a psychologist...." and, *Twilight* opens with: "Idleness is the beginning of all psychology."

Self-culture was another goal, and to this end, conventional morality was considered a constraint. In contrast, there was Nietzsche's much-repeated quotation by Ancient Greek poet, Pindar: *Become who you are.* This may very well have been Wilde's mantra. "The contemplative life, the life that has for its aim not *doing* but *being*, and not *being* merely, but *becoming*—this is what the critical spirit can give us," Wilde writes in his essay *The Critic as Artist*.

In the words of Wilde, it was personalities and not principles that moved the age and the development of the race depended on the development of the individual. Nietzsche, too, believed unswervingly in the primacy of the individual, or his 'higher men.' It was the few who made history, and changed the world and thus the aim of mankind lay with them. With their perfervid individualism, both believed in great men, as they believed in themselves; and liked to imagine themselves as grand historical personages, and to recreate the great in their own image. In *De Profundis*, Wilde comes dangerously close to posing as Jesus Christ, who in turn is resurrected as the premiere Romantic poet; while Socrates and Shakespeare as reconceived by Nietzsche sound a great deal like himself. Of Shakespeare, Nietzsche writes "what must a man have suffered to find it so very necessary to be a buffoon" while Socrates is distinguished by "the gay kind of seriousness and that *wisdom full of pranks.*"

But, in escaping from all systems and declaring war on all mores and moral valuations, what they forged could be unsettling. For one, truth was relative. In Nietzsche's Notebooks, *Will to Power*, we read: "Facts is precisely what there is not, only interpretations." This is Perspectivism, a position that suggests that any worldview, the scientific included, is only one outlook among others. In *Beyond Good and Evil* he writes, "supposing that this is also only interpretation—and you will be eager enough to make this objection?—well, so much the better." Wilde agreed with this theory of relativity (moral or otherwise).

One of his paradoxes from *A Few Maxims for the Instruction of the Overeducated* had it: "When a truth becomes a fact, it loses all its intellectual value." Yet Man, they agreed, could not live without illusions. Nietzsche especially was relentless in his defense of, and insistence on, our psychological need for myth. Life, first, at any cost, meant recognizing untruth as a condition of life, (self) deception as sometimes necessary, or a partial shutting of one eye to better see with the other. Thus, their advocacy of life-sustaining illusions was as much a plea for the exercising of imagination as for self-enhancement, since they were in the service of life.

Being great contrarians meant standing everything on its head, and taking unconscionable positions. In his essay, *The Soul of Man under Socialism*, Wilde promotes a gentle anarchy or, "doing what one likes;" and, in conversation he went so far as to say, only half in jest, that whenever anyone agrees with him, he felt he must be wrong. Meanwhile, as late as 1878-79, Nietzsche confided to a friend that he had no philosophical thought of his own. In all earnestness—without joke or provocation—he volunteered that his idea of a method was to contrast what was currently valid, as all new teachings contained a reversal of one or more old ones. The subtitle for Nietzsche's *Zarathustra* is a case in point of his contrarian impulse: *a book for all and a book for none.*

To make matters worse, they contradicted themselves, wildly. A running joke among Nietzsche scholars is: pick any statement he makes, if you cannot find a passage where he contradicts it, you have not looked hard enough. Or, as a German satirist once quipped: "Tell me what you need, and I'll supply you with the right Nietzsche quotation." And, in fact, with his ability to lend himself to innumerable interpretations, Nietzsche especially has been claimed by almost everyone: Anarchists, Atheists, Christians, Fascists, Liberals, Postmodernists, Deconstructionists, Existentialists, Rationalists, Irrationalists, Positivists and Nihilists. Wilde too had something to say to everyone on everything. As Dorothy Parker noted in her witty ditty:

If, with the literate, I am

Impelled to try an epigram,

I never seek to take the credit;

We all assume that Oscar said it.

Ironically, this broad appeal did not ensure comprehension, or in the words of Hegel: "What is well known is not necessarily known merely because it is well known." For, in addition to Nietzsche and Wilde's theater of contradictions—already fraught with ambiguities and ornate stylistic evasions—their skepticism, irony and ambivalence compounded the difficulty of knowing where they stood in relation to their (often extreme) positions. In defense of his preference for ambiguity, and ability to champion diametrically opposite notions, Wilde had written in a letter to parodist and novelist Ada Leverson: "God and other artists are always a little obscure." Being facetious in *Dorian Gray*, at the expense of religion, morality, etc...Lord Henry Wotton-cum-Wilde is asked to state his position. He replies: "Threads tear, you would get lost in the labyrinth." Likewise, Nietzsche, who spoke of the 'incommunicability of the heart', was inscrutable even in his personal correspondences. According to distinguished critic and translator, Christopher Middleton, "the letters are like aerial photography of a subterranean labyrinth." Those who knew him, personally, also confessed to feeling in the presence of a riddle or mystery. Furthermore, philosophically, it was one of Nietzsche's central doctrines that personality was without a fixed core or essence.

"I contradict myself? Very well, then, I contradict myself. I am vast. I contain multitudes" wrote Walt Whitman. Aristotle concurs; according to him, a mark of an educated person is the ability to hold contradictory thoughts in mind at the same time, and not be discomfited. Wilde and Nietzsche were vast and 'educated' in this manner. Both confessed to housing (at least) three selves, each. Nietzsche, who relished the art of statement and counterstatement, wrote in *Beyond Good and Evil*: "Our body is but a social structure composed of many souls." In conversation with Lou Salome, an attractive, intellectual Russian woman (only 21 when Nietzsche was smitten with her at 37) he describes himself as a tertium quid, a disembodied third person or entity.

'It composes,' he says, 'I am neither mind nor body but another dimensional entity.'

Wilde's formulation is less mystical, yet he also thinks of himself in multiples. "I am certain that I have three separate souls … for in addition to the counter urges, there is a third urge to contemplate the other two." Both likened their souls to a 'stringed instrument.' Wilde in an early poem, "Helas," sings: "To drift with every passion till my soul/ Is a stringed lute on which all winds can play." The same image is in Nietzsche's "Gondola Song," a late poem which appears untitled in his autobiography. On the night train to the Basel psychiatric clinic, following his mental collapse, he burst into song (from his *Gondola* poem): "And my soul, a stringed instrument/ sang, touched by invisible hands."

From a scientific standpoint, Danish physicist Niels Bohr suggests that there are two kinds of truth: "there are the superficial truths, the opposite of which are obviously wrong. But there are also the profound truths, whose opposites are equally right." In his essay, "The Truth of Masks," Wilde had made a similar assertion, "a truth in art is that whose contradiction is also true." At the end of that essay, Wilde offers a diversionary paradox, as was his method: "Not that I agree with everything that I have said in this essay…There is much with which I entirely disagree." Nietzsche, too, agrees to disagree with himself, reserving at all times the right to counter argue, as a philosopher's birthright: "A thinker needs no one to refute him. He is quite capable of doing that himself." A man of many "moods" who wrote through all of them, his views shifted dramatically; a position he cleverly justified in his aphorism that "every philosophy is the philosophy of some stage of life." Or, more elaborately, in a psychological confession, entitled *Short Habits*, "I always believe that this particular thing will give me permanent satisfaction…and one day its time is over… That is how it goes for me with foods, thoughts, people, cities…ways of life."

Nietzsche's fluctuating appreciation of the role of art and the artist is a prime example of his restless, changeable mind. Depending on his mood, and resisting his own musical and lyrical impulses, the artist could be portrayed as visionary prophet or romantic charlatan. In his early work, the ecstatic-florid *Birth of Tragedy*, we are told that "it is only as an aesthetic phenomenon that existence is justified." But, by his middle period, the rational-scientific *Human, All Too Human*, Nietzsche has changed his mind. "Regarding truths, the artist has a weaker morality than the thinker." In later life, in a letter to Georg Brandes, eminent Danish critic and the first to lecture on him *during* his sane life, Nietzsche plainly confesses "we philosophers are grateful to be mistaken for artists."

Wilde's oscillating appreciation for nature is a similar instance of this mental malleability. As a poet he sang the praises of nature, as a critic he rejected it (for "lack of design") in favor of art, and as an artist he returned to it for inspiration.

Pain Threshold

Wilde emerged from prison a man with a broken will. To the repeated inducements by his devoted friend and brave biographer Frank Harris that he should write, Wilde admitted that he could not, since he was born to sing of life's joy and not sorrow. To Andre Gide's mild reproach for not writing (and letting himself go), he replied: "One shouldn't be angry with someone who has been struck." Only pity (for others) had kept him from killing himself in prison, he confided to Gide. But after his great song of pity, *Ballad of Reading Gaol*, the rest is silence. There were half-hearted creative miscarriages and aborted ideas for plays (*Pharaoh, Ahab and Jezebel*), yet his last works of fiction were his letters, whose gaiety was largely artificial and their bold surface joy masked the angst beneath. There would be one last self-invention, however, the pseudonym he adopted after prison living in Paris: Sebastian Melmoth, fusing a martyred saint with a Faustian hero of Gothic Romance.

In prison, he had written the rousing words: "I have got to make everything that has happened to me good for me…each and all of these things I have to transform into a spiritual exercise." Such affirmation and talk of spiritual alchemy sounds a great deal like Nietzsche's 'formula for greatness in a human being,' *amor fati*, namely "that one wants nothing to be different…not merely bear what is necessary, still less to conceal it…but love it." Yet, Wilde would not follow through on his promises to himself, and in fact, this was one of the chief differences

between Nietzsche and Wilde: their relation
or response to suffering.

With a will that he describes in *Zarathustra*
as an "uninjurable, unburiable force" and
"a cliff leaping stream," Nietzsche was
the braver spiritual warrior. Because of
his physical condition and psychological
disposition, his "specialty was to endure pain"
as he writes in a letter to Brandes. Living as
he did for several years 'in close proximity
to death,' Nietzsche certainly had the higher
pain threshold (physical and spiritual). What
he has written on pain, could fill a small
book. Here he is in praise of pain: "Profound
suffering ennobles. It sets apart." In *The Gay
Science*, he informs us "I have just given a
name to my pain and call it "dog." It is just as
faithful, just as obtrusive and shameless, just
as entertaining, just as clever as any other
dog." Justly proud of having found a way to
transform and benefit from suffering, there is
more affirmation of its value in Nietzsche.

For this reason, he writes: "To those human beings who are of any concern to me I wish suffering, desolation, sickness, ill-treatment, indignities—I wish that they should not remain unfamiliar with profound self-contempt, the torture of self-mistrust, the wretchedness of the vanquished: I have no pity for them, because I wish them the only thing that can prove today whether one is worth anything or not—that one endures." For endure he does, all forms of suffering and indignities, to realize in an epilogue of one of his last books: *Nietzsche Contra Wagner*: "I have often asked myself whether I am not more heavily obligated to the hardest years of my life than to others...I doubt that such a pain makes us 'better', but I know that it makes us more *profound*."

Personal Struggle

The discrepancies between the private face and the public façade were considerable, however. Past style, there were personal struggles, and personas fraying. If there are structural weaknesses in Wilde or Nietzsche's thinking, it is because the edifice of their philosophies appears to be built on a fault line. To better understand the pressures behind the writing, one must consider where the stresses fall in their lives. For example, though both address themselves to life, it was truly in art where they immersed themselves and fled into a kind of mystic ecstasy. "Body and soul, I am more of a battlefield than a human being," Nietzsche admitted. Wilde too was riddled with warring impulses. Paradoxically, despite their almost aggressive individualism, both viewed the self as something to be mistrusted or feared, seeking to transcend the personal and dissolve or diffuse their personalities through the deployment of personas, or masks. Their contrariness encompassed both an assertion of the self as well as a denial of it. "Promise me: from now on don't ever write I anymore," Wilde told Gide, commenting on his book *Fruits of the Earth*. "In art, there is no *first* person."

Profoundly antagonistic to what was most profoundly related to him, Nietzsche struggled violently with, and denounced loudly, what was deeply rooted in him or what he possessed in excess, namely: pity, piety, morality. In *Conversations with Nietzsche*, Lou Salome (whom he referred to as his 'twin soul') noted at the very beginning of their acquaintance (1882) that he was of a religious nature. Years later, she wrote: "Today I would want to underscore this expression doubly…We will experience it yet that he will step forth as the proclaimer of a new religion, and then it will be such a one as recruits heroes to be its disciples." In fact, this was what she felt would lead him to his *Zarathustra*: "the deep movement of the God-seeker … who came from religion and was heading toward religious prophecy." Of *Salome*, the self-styled 'immoralist' would write in a draft of a letter to their mutual friend, moral philosopher Paul Ree: "She told me herself that she had no morality—and I thought she had, like myself, a more severe morality than anybody." Finally, Nietzsche's collapse in the streets of Turin, insane, as he wept with his arms flung around a tired old horse to shield it from whipping, is a pathetic portrait of pity.

Nietzsche's caustic remarks on asceticism, weakness, and idealism, or his vitriol for German culture in general, are best understood in this framework as well: as inner threats. For example, despite often highly-charged sexual metaphors, and his condemnation of the preaching of celibacy as a sin against life, his life remained essentially sexless. Likewise, for all his vaunted celebration of Dionysus or his repeated praise for dancing, he neither drank nor

43

danced (although during the insane years he practiced some form of impressionist dance).

Nietzsche's mad letters make for particularly horrible reading—heavens rejoicing and everything transfigured, the landscape populated with satyrs and festival animals—because we suspect that only in madness was he able to realize his ideal of the 'god who dances.' Always a more commanding writer than speaker, the two faculties appear to have fused during the early months of his insanity. Shortly after his mental collapse in 1889, in a Jena psychiatric clinic, Nietzsche is exhibited to a classroom of medical students. One of the students notes: "We had never heard a man speak this way…I had just felt the magic power of the Nietzsche style for the first time. For he spoke as he wrote: short sentences full of peculiar word combinations and elaborate antitheses."

Despite longing to be a 'Good European'

throughout his life—claiming ties to Polish nobility, or that he was closest to the Italians, or that his subtle personality could only be at home in Paris—Nietzsche remained more of a bad German, never quite shaking off the Idealism he damned them for. Despite peppering his writing with French, German was the only language he spoke. And, in spite of excursions to Switzerland and Italy (he never did visit Paris) he could never stay away from Germany for long, returning regularly for bitter winters and family feuds (which occasioned the sour comment, "those nearest to me are changed into ulcers.") Even stylistically, he was more German than he would bear to hear. Although he could soar high with incandescent prose, for all his talk of "light feet" and despite often felicitous phrasing, when he came down, he came down awfully hard, strident and severe; or in his own words "radical to the point of criminality."

Failures as Wicked Men

In the same vein as Nietzsche, who privately worried that perhaps he wished to be more of a free spirit than he could, Wilde, fascinated as he was by wickedness, admits to being a failure as a wicked man. In a letter to the *Scots Observer* (1890) defending the "immorality" of *Dorian Gray*, Wilde repeated a claim he had made in the preface of that novel: "An artist has no ethical sympathies," adding "virtue and wickedness are to him simply what the colors on his palette are to the painter." And yet the person who penned this seems to have disagreed. For all its wicked surface dazzle, *Portrait of Dorian Gray*, was a cautionary tale with a plain moral, in the words of Pater: "[that] vice and crime make people coarse and ugly." And the man Wilde was as morally conflicted as his protagonist, Dorian, who comes undone in the novel when Lord Henry flippantly recounts overhearing a man in the street recite from the Bible, "What profit a man if he gain the whole world, and lose his own soul?"

Throughout his only novel, it appears Wilde was warning himself of himself, only he was confessing over his own head, in the very sense that Nietzsche meant when he wrote that 'every philosophy or morality was an unconscious or involuntary memoir.' In *The Importance of Being Earnest*, subtitled 'a trivial comedy for serious people,' he has Jack confess "it is a terrible thing for a man to find out suddenly that all his life he has been speaking nothing but the truth." In his reminiscences on Oscar Wilde, Andre Gide also stresses the importance of the plays as "confidences," or in what they reveal about the author to "him whose ears are sharp." Certainly, the Wilde of *De Profundis* was not *beyond good and evil* when he confesses, "What the paradox was to me in the sphere of thought, perversity became to me in the sphere of passion. Desire, at the end, was a malady, or a madness, or both." In the same way, his last poem, *Ballad of Reading Gaol* is a work of contrition:

And the wild regrets, and the bloody sweats,
None knew so well as I:
For he who lives more lives than one
More deaths than one must die.

In Max Nordau's intemperate attack on 19th century culture—a work that is at best caustic criticism but deteriorates into spite and spittle—Wilde and Nietzsche (along with Baudelaire, Swinburne, and Wagner) are labeled degenerates. 'Degenerate,' in this context, is defined as 'morbid deviation… containing transmissible elements.' Nietzsche fell under "Decadents and Aesthetes" in the section on "Egomania;" reportedly suffering from 'contradiction mania' and 'pronounced

sadism,' only with him it was confined
to the intellectual sphere, according to
Herr Nordau. Meanwhile, Wilde who
kept Nietzsche company in the section
on Egomania, was additionally guilty of
apparently admiring "immorality, sin and
crime."

But, as with most criticism, if we overlook
its rabid accents, there appears to be a kernel
of truth. In prison, Wilde confessed that
desire had become a malady and in an appeal
to the Home Secretary (1896) he pitifully
cites the 'eminent man of science, Nordau,'
in excusing "sexual madness" as a "disease to
be cured by a physician rather than a crime
to be punished by a judge." Meanwhile,
Nietzsche, who was much preoccupied with
questions of decadence, could be regarded as
self-damning in his own definition of literary
decadence as an 'anarchy of atoms,' where the
whole is no longer a whole and the thinking
is fragmented.

Wilde and Nietzsche both embodied *fin de siecle malaise* and its signature disease, in that both were most likely syphilitic; Nietzsche's mental collapse and degenerative paralysis were in all probability brought on by tertiary syphilis. Possessed of a latent fatality, both were self-destructive and attracted to tragedy; Nietzsche's extreme discipline and asceticism, for example, could often look like masochism. Each wrestled with *Eros* and *Thanatos* in their own ways, as they cynically flirted with nihilism and personal abysses. Having met Wilde, Gide admitted, "[Reading] Nietzsche astonished me less, later on, because I had heard Wilde say: 'Not happiness! Above all, not happiness. Pleasure! We must always want the most tragic…'"

Dangerous Legacy
Yet, in spite of several parallels in their projects and the projection of their

personalities, as thinkers they are not of the same order of difficulty or scope of interest. Though perhaps the least systematic of philosophers and the most literary, Nietzsche's project far more than Wilde's, made self-overcoming and transformation its concern and commitment. Furthermore, as a professional thinker, Nietzsche's range, sphere of thought and influence were wider and deeper than those of Wilde's. For this reason, in considering the question of influence, we must momentarily set Wilde aside.

Having already touched on the various disciplines and movements that have appropriated Nietzsche—Existentialism, literary criticism and psychoanalysis— it is worthwhile to mention also that, exceptionally among philosophers, he has inspired scores of musicians (over 200). Moreover, he has profoundly influenced literary figures of such stature as Rilke,

Hesse, Mann, Shaw and Gide to name but a few. One suspects that this would not have surprised him much. Equally, he predicted his negative influence with uncanny prescience. Having completed *Zarathustra*, Nietzsche anticipates his dangerous legacy, in a letter to author and patron Malwida von Meysenbug (1884): "...I am appalled by the thought of all the unqualified and wholly unsuitable types who will someday appeal to my authority. But this is the torment of every great teacher of mankind: he knows that he has as much chance of becoming its curse as its blessing."

In examining his influence on two modern thinkers, we see the problem in microcosm. Heidegger and Foucault's Nietzschean fixation and inheritance are more insidious than they may first appear. The reality of Foucault's application of Nietzsche's abstract injunction to "Live dangerously [and] build your cities on the slopes of

Vesuvius" is AIDS, according to James Miller's disquieting *The Passion of Michel Foucault*. Foucault, who expressed a deep and abiding interest in the unholy trinity of madness, perversity and crime, had morbidly volunteered in an interview: "I would like and I hope I'll die of an overdose of pleasure of any kind."

Nietzsche's actual application of this volcanic philosophy is questionable—the self-styled immoralist who lived like a monk, the prophet-like "Anti-Christ" who pronounced God dead and sought to found a new religion. Though Nietzsche was fundamentally anti-political, Thomas Mann does not entirely absolve him of Nazi misappropriation. Instead, Mann associates him with the "guilt of the intellect, its unpolitical disregard of the actual world, surrender to the esthetic enjoyment of its own audacities…" More to the point, Nietzschean concepts such as the *Overman* (while an overman of the spirit) and the *Will to Power* (implying power over oneself) lend themselves to practical misinterpretations, or worse still, misapplications.

"Mankind sacrificed en masse so that one single stronger species of man might thrive— that would be progress" What to make of such an incendiary bit of theoretical cruelty, from *Genealogy of Morals?* Or again, how to account for this fanciful falsehood: "The errors of great men are venerable because they are more fruitful than the truths of little men." Ultimately, even a coinage such as "beyond good and evil" if it is not dismissed altogether as "esthetic enjoyment of its own audacities," may seem only permissible in theory. Witness Heidegger's grotesque and shameful association with the Nazis, another Nietzschean philosopher incapable of differentiating between the irresponsible idea and the responsible reality. Hannah Arendt, student and lover of Heidegger, blamed his Nazism on incorrigible romanticism, "a spiritual playfulness that stems in part from delusions of grandeur and in part from despair." In this indulgent and generous analysis, Arendt may as well have been delineating Nietzsche's temperament, and excusing him of all his reckless rhetorical excesses in the process.

Personally reserved and awkwardly shy, Nietzsche compensated himself through such self-aggrandizement and thundering prose, alternating between the hyperbolic and the histrionic. ('A gentle man in every way…a lion at the desk' in the words of one of his landlords). His bombastic remark "I am not a man, I am dynamite," was probably lifted from a book review of *Beyond Good and Evil*, one of precious few reviews during his conscious life. Here is an excerpt: "Spiritual explosives, like material ones, can do very useful work; it is not necessary that they be abused for criminal purposes. Yet one does well to label such stuff carefully: This is dynamite." Everything considered, it is not surprising that he should have been inordinately pleased with this comparison, and would later write in his notebooks: "Terribleness belongs to greatness, let us not deceive ourselves."

This is the artist-thinker as theoretical monster, capable of negative inspiration or leading astray. In *Conversations with Kafka*, Kafka is presented with Wilde's *Intentions* (a volume of essays) and says: 'It sparkles and seduces…And that is one of the books great dangers…because it plays with the truth. A game with truth is always a game with life."

Unfortunately, such criticism also applies to Nietzsche, who was far from invulnerable to playing such truth games. In the words of the seminal Nietzsche scholar Walter Kaufmann, "Nietzsche had an almost pathological weakness for one particular kind of ambiguity…he loved words or phrases that mean one thing out of context and almost the opposite in the context he gives them in."

Plays on words were also plays on ideas, or 'games with truth and life.' Thus Nietzsche and Wilde courted misunderstandings, or cultivated misinterpretations, that when not detrimental to others were harmful to their own reputations. In this way, they provided the superficial reader with an excuse to dismiss them as poseurs, associated not with serious philosophies but a clutch of special effects. In his introduction to the *Portable Nietzsche* Kaufmann rightly points out: "He could not resist a *bon mot* or a striking coinage, and he took delight in inventing better slogans and epigrams for hostile positions than his opponents could devise."

Temptations of the Aphorist
Perhaps this is a particularly great temptation

to resist for the writer of aphorisms, epigrams, or maxims, since it is a risk inherent in the form. As apparently isolated fragments, aphoristic or epigrammatic writing is especially susceptible to readings out of context. Another danger perhaps inherent in the form is the generalizing impulse. However electrifying or startling the observation, the philosopher's arrogance in summarizing is implicit; it is a finality that brooks no exceptions. And, as the last word on a given subject, aphorisms could be viewed as intolerant little formulations that paved the way for violent misunderstanding.

But Nietzsche and Wilde were aware that living against the grain of themselves and the times was a situation humanly untenable, and that they could not last. Nietzsche who signed early letters, "a young old man, who bears no grudge against life, but must long for the end," confessed in 1885 to Franz Overbeck, his closest friend and a professor of church history, "My life now consists in the wish that it might be otherwise with all things than I comprehend, and that somebody might make my 'truths' appear incredible to me…" Playing a dangerous guessing game that same year, author Paul Lansky asks Nietzsche to divine his future. Nietzsche spoke with an almost trembling voice: "It cannot be, I do not want to believe it, but …, but … I fear you will go crazy … if you do not take your own life." Lansky was horror-stricken and when it was his turn to predict the philosopher's supposed fate, said: "I thought the same of you." Nietzsche answered with a smile, "So it will be I?" adding, calmly "I…will die by my own hand…when my hour will come." As we know, he was not to die by his own hand, but to slip into irretrievable insanity less than four years later.

Coleridge, another philosophical poet and kindred spirit, praised in his *Biographia Literaria* 'men in all ages who have been impelled by instinct to propose their own nature as a problem, and who devoted their attempts to its solution.' Wilde had remarked that he was a problem for which there was no solution, and it can be said that Nietzsche's life was devoted to the solution of his 'nature as a problem.' Yet, both arrived at the end of their tether, experiencing *taedium vitae* (world weariness) from opposite ends of the spectrum; Nietzsche's was theoretical and rooted in abstinence, Wilde's experiential and derived from excess.

On a trip to Algeria, a frenzied Wilde declares to Gide, before embarking to England and rushing headlong into harm: "I must go as far as possible...I cannot go further...something must happen... something else." That something else, Gide remarks darkly in his memories of Wilde: "was hard labor." Concurring with Gide, after prison, that he had foreseen the danger to a certain extent, Wilde exclaimed: "Oh! Of course! Of course! I knew that there would be a catastrophe—that one or another, I was expecting it. It had to end that way. Just imagine: it wasn't possible to go any further; and it couldn't last. That's why, you see, it has to be ended."

In an earlier letter to Scottish writer-adventurer R.B. Cunningham Graham, Wilde had written: "I . . . wish we could talk over the many prisons of life prisons of stone, prisons of passion, prisons of intellect, prisons of morality and the rest all limitations, external or internal, all prisons, really. All life is a limitation." Behind bars he also wrote: "I know that on the day of my release I shall be merely passing from one prison to another." This world view of life as limitation, or vast prison, was shared by Nietzsche and informed both men's extravagant life-responses and desperate attempts to forge a new world where they might live more freely.

Experiments with Values

Vaguely grudging Wilde's wide fame and posthumous status as a martyr, Shaw indulges in a hypothetical exercise: how would Wilde be presented to posterity had he died before his tragedy (i.e. scandal and imprisonment)? In his estimation: "Oscar would still have been remembered as a wit and a dandy, and would have had a niche beside Congreve in theater history. A volume of his aphorisms would have stood creditably on the library shelf with La Rouchefoucauld's *Maxims*."

What of Nietzsche, then, minus his martyrdom and tragedy (i.e. if he had died sane)? It is difficult to predict. Still, it is more difficult to imagine such universal celebrity (with all its distorting mirrors) for a philosopher, however unorthodox his method or dazzling his style. Safe to say,

Nietzsche would still have cut a dashing figure in the halls of both literature and psychology and had a niche beside modern philosophers—given the controversy beginning to surround his name during his last conscious year, as well as the modest success of the Brandes lectures introducing him to an international audience.

In assessing both Wilde and Nietzsche one must concede that at times, they came close to discrediting themselves through their tendency toward hyperbole. The desire to shock-into-truth was sometimes displaced by the less noble desire to simply shock, which is the difference between holding someone's attention and grabbing it. Yet, even their half truths, if they did not always impart sustenance or give pleasure, communicated enthusiasms, and could excite contemplation. Certainly such verbal pyrotechnics were not for the morally squeamish, nor the fiercely independent, poetical-philosophical creed they propagated. Depending on the indulgence of the reader, responses have varied from astonishment to amusement to exasperation.

Whether celebrated as liberators or maligned as pernicious influences, Nietzsche and Wilde could be insolent, reckless or reactionary in their defiant assault upon accepted norms, beliefs, customs, etc...That is why we must consult them cautiously, suspiciously even, the way we would precocious children toying with ideas, or court-jesters spewing an often mad wisdom. Like children too, they had the habit of destroying their own toys, thereby leaving us with what we brought to the table, somewhat rattled. In *Other Inquisitions*, Borges writes of Wilde: "He gave the century what the century demanded—*comedies larmoyantes* [tearjerker comedies] for the many, and verbal arabesques for the few—and he executed those dissimilar things with a kind of negligent glee."

Possibly, as master stylists, they wrote too well for their own good, and allowed themselves to be maddened by their own texts, or intoxicated with their own eloquence. Highly attuned as they were to the musicality of words, they may at times have permitted style to dictate content, or eclipse substance. In a letter written in 1884 to an old friend, Erwin Rohde, Nietzsche confesses: "My style is a dance, it plays with all sorts of symmetries, only to leap over and scoff at them. This applies even to the choice of vowels." In turn, Gide's critique of Wilde's style could apply to Nietzsche: 'the glittering of the surface makes our mind lose sight of the deep central emotion.' Shaw seconded this sentiment, regarding Wilde, and slightly amended it: "[He] was so in love with style, that he never realized the danger…of putting up more style than his matter would carry."

The danger of laying on more style than the matter would carry is an occupational hazard of ventriloquists. Capable of fantastic impersonations, they can throw their voices everywhere, and make it sound like it came from anywhere, except their own mouths. While appearing to move mountains with their high-flying pronouncements, Nietzsche and Wilde often cowered behind their blustering bravado and outsized slippery style, doing violence to themselves in the process by arguing what they did not necessarily mean, or appearing to say more than they would personally back.

As extremists, both recognized the truth that extremes are closer to one another than the middle path, or moderation, which so eluded them. Or, in Nietzsche's words, "Extreme positions are not succeeded by moderate ones, but by contrary extreme positions." In *Will to Power*, he elaborates: "The spell that fights on our behalf, the Venus eye that charms and blinds even our opponents, is *the magic of the extreme*, the seduction that everything extreme exercises: we immoralists—we are the most extreme." Both were bewitched by extremity in this way and, in seeing both sides of an argument at once, occasionally risked becoming philosophically cross-eyed. The result was a thinking that not only appeared to be profoundly confusing, but also profoundly confused.

Ultimately, both were philosophers in the Socratic sense, in that they raised more questions than they answered. These questing spirits, interrogated the value of traditional answers in determining how we live and what we think we know. In *Schopenhauer as Teacher*, Nietzsche had written: "I care for a philosopher only to the extent that he is able to be an example..." This is what emerges from the texts of Nietzsche and Wilde. Each in their own unusual way managed to create of themselves a prodigious example, or a living sign, entrusting to posterity their peculiar personalities, of which their works are only a part. Overlooking his written work, and focusing on Wilde the gifted storyteller and brilliant talker, Gide characterized him as: "a great *viveur* ... like the philosophers of Greece, Wilde did not write but talked and lived his wisdom..."

In Wilde's trial, somewhat echoing Socrates' trial for thinking differently and 'corrupting the youth,' Wilde's own words were used against him and he was cross-examined on the usefulness to youth of his "Phrases and Philosophies for the Use of the Young," a collection of paradoxical maxims on wickedness, religion, truth, pleasure and perfection. On the subject of "corruption," Nietzsche has this to say in his *Dawn*: "The surest way to corrupt a youth is to instruct him to hold in higher esteem those who think alike than those who think differently."

Justifying his involvement with a writer or

thinker (in this case, Nietzsche) Danish critic
Georg Brandes writes: "my first question
is this: What is the value of this man, is he
interesting, or not? If he is, then his books
are undoubtedly worth knowing. Questions
of right or wrong are seldom applicable in
the highest intellectual spheres...We are not
children in search of instruction, but skeptics
in search of men." This is a mature position
to adopt towards both Nietzsche and Wilde.
Certainly they are interesting, whether or
not they were right or wrong. The question
of their value is a larger one. Undoubtedly,
we do not find them as outrageous as they
were to their 19th century sensibility.
Rather, in our age, skeptical of absolutes and
susceptible to pluralism of interpretations,
we consider them contemporaries, or
modern diagnosticians whose experiments
with values mirror our own. Even in their
contradictory works we recognize, writ
large, the wonderful and complex workings

of the human psyche. Thus as agents of regeneration who live on in us, their currency renews their value—rendering them, at the very least, as relevant today as they were over a century ago.

Appreciation

As pithy and erudite as his subjects, Yahia Lababidi presents a meeting of the minds that highlights the weight of Wilde's famous wit and the levity behind Nietzsche's tragic insights.
— Jeremy Richards, author of *"Nietzsche! The Musical"*

Thanks for your brilliant essay on Wilde and Nietzsche. They're two people I read, but it's never occurred to me to put them together (I've never seen anyone else do it either) and it really works, right down to the aphorisms. It's an invigorating piece, passionate and exact, and headlong in momentum, a real pleasure.
— James Richardson, Professor Emeritus of Creative Writing at Princeton University, poet, and aphorist.

I thank you for your fine piece on Wilde and Nietzsche, the "Contrarians". Nietzsche and

Wilde are not usually brought together and discussed so thoughtfully.
— David Krell, Professor Emeritus of Philosophy at DePaul University, novelist and Nietzsche scholar.

I think your Wilde and Nietzsche essay excellent. Your mind has a far-ranging quality, a tendency to see parallels that others would not see, which reminds me of my own.

My first reaction …that comparing Wilde and Nietzsche is like comparing a meringue with a five-course dinner….But your essay certainly made me feel that you have justified the comparison and said some very interesting things, showing a remarkable talent and originality.

A fascinating piece, that would make any intelligent person aware that you are a person of considerable intellectual voltage…
— Colin Wilson, existential philosopher and author of *The Outsider*.

About the Author

Yahia Lababidi, Arab-American of
Palestinian background, is the author of 13
critically-acclaimed books. Lababidi has
been called "our greatest living aphorist" and
a "current-day master" of this ancient form.
His prose and poetry meditations have gone
viral, are used in classrooms and religious
services, and are featured at international
festivals.

Lababidi has contributed to news, literary and cultural institutions throughout the USA, Europe and the Middle East, such as: Oxford University, Pearson Education, PBS NewsHour, NPR, HBO & ABC Radio.

Lababidi's latest works include: *What Remains To Be Said* (Wild Goose Publications, 2025) new & selected aphorisms of his composed over the past three decades, as well as *Palestine Wail* (Daraja Press, 2024) a love letter to Gaza in response to the ongoing Genocide.

www.ingramcontent.com/pod-product-compliance
Lightning Source LLC
Chambersburg PA
CBHW020414150626
46554CB00013B/966